TIMELESS LIVING

1995-2005

TIMELESS LIVING

1995-2005

BETA-PLUS

FOREWORD

At the end of 1995, we made our first photo reports for the book *Construire avec la pierre naturelle* (Building with Natural Stone), the first title in a thematic collection of architecture and interiors books.

Ten years later, the series consists of thirty titles, each of which has informed the reader about an aspect of construction or design: *Le Bois dans l'Habitat* (Living with Wood), *Construire avec des matériaux anciens* (Building with Old Materials), *Vivre avec les Antiquités* (Living with Antiques), *Couleur et habitat* (Colour in the House), *Vivre et travailler* (Living and Working), *Vivre avec l'Art* (Living with Art), *Cuisines intemporelles* (Timeless Kitchens), *Salles de bains intemporelles* (Timeless Bathrooms), *Maisons de vacances* (Holiday Homes), *Intérieurs intemporels* (Timeless Interiors) and *Jardins intemporels* (Timeless Gardens).

These books were published only in French and Dutch.
Many of the titles are already in their second or third edition, and more than half of the publications are sold out. For these reasons we have decided to publish this special anthology.

Timeless Living 1995-2005 contains a compilation of the most inspiring reports from the past decade, arranged by theme: the most beautiful entrance halls, drawing rooms, dining rooms, kitchens, bathrooms, bedrooms and dressing rooms, rooms for relaxation and for work, and everything around the house.

The book concludes with an up-to-date list of weblinks for the architects, interior specialists, craftspeople, manufacturers and distributors who are presented in this unique publication.

We would like to thank our many readers for their years of support and hope that leafing through this anthology will provide them with as much inspiration and information as our previous publications.

Wim Pauwels
Publisher

CONTENTS

ENTRANCE HALLS

The entrance hall represents the link between the outside world and the interior of the house.
Functionality and aesthetic aspects go hand in hand here:
the durability of the selected materials is of prime importance,
but the character and the arrangement of these rooms is also of key concern.
The hall leads the visitor into the house and, from an architectural point of view,
it is often the basis that all the living spaces are built around.

The old bluestone slabs and the wrought-iron door were supplied by *Group Moris*.

Francis Van Damme installed this old Burgundian curved door that leads to a sanitary room.

In this entrance hall, created by *Group Moris*, reclaimed bluestone slabs have been combined with *Corical* lime paints.

A design by architect *Bernard De Clerck*. Old floors in black marble and white Carrara marble.

The entrance hall in a country home, restored in collaboration with *Raymond Rombouts*.
To the left is a work by *Michel Mouffe*.

A monochrome colour palette in natural shades, combined with austere forms in this villa restored by architect *Vincent Van Duysen*.

A Basaltina lavastone floor creates a sense of continuity and is in harmony with the minimal style of *Filip Van Bever*. Natural stone works: *Van Den Weghe*.

Two projects by interior designer *Gert Voorjans*.

A view of the summer sitting room in a restored nineteenth-century farmhouse. Design by *Polyèdre*.

In these three projects by architect *Stéphane Boens*, *Rik Storms'* historical construction materials have been integrated to create a whole that is timeless and exclusive.

The stairs (picture on the left) were constructed from old oak beams.

The entrance hall of the restored brewery owned by the antique-dealers *Michel and Christine Ceuterick*.

The minimalist atmosphere of a contemporary home. The entrance hall has been painted with lime paints by *Bert de Waal*.

A design by architect *Xavier Donck*. The antique furnishings and other items were selected by the antique-dealer *Garnier*.

Contemporary art in an entrance hall designed by architect *Stéphane Boens*.

A brushed parquet floor with wide boards has been tinted with oil (*Saillart*).

SITTING ROOMS

Drawing rooms, or sitting rooms, usually have a dual function: they are used to receive guests,
but also for resting and calming down after a hard day's work.
The great variety of sitting rooms in this chapter reveals this ambiguity: from formal to relaxed,
from opulent to extremely minimal – a choice that is reflected
in the selection of furnishings, materials and of the colour palette.

Two designs by the antique-dealer and interior specialist *Axel Vervoordt*.

The walls of the orangery (picture on the right) have been painted with lime paints by *Dankers Decor* in order to achieve an aged

effect. A tadelakt adds the finishing touch to the fireplace. A monolithic 'Pastelone' floor: a mix of brick dust and limestone.

Some seating designs by *Axel Vervoordt* in Kanaal, Wijnegem.

PP. 44-45

An interior created by *Axel Vervoordt* in the centre of Ghent.

The deep *Brian* settee has a loose cover.

The coffee table is an old door

that has been placed on a simple metal frame.

A *Howard Club* armchair.

The old Versailles parquet has been sanded white.

PP. 46-47

Vervoordt again, in a lovely seaside villa: the seating and
furnishings are by the world-famous Antwerp antique-dealer.

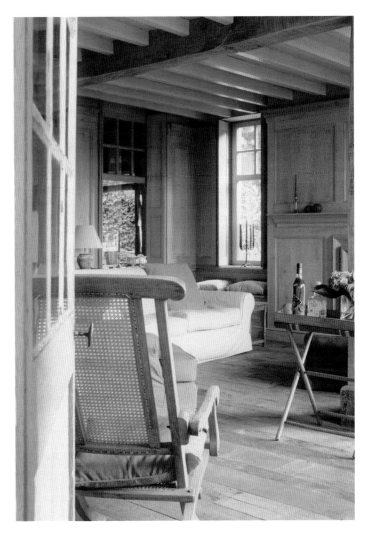

A *Walda Pairon* design.

The old wooden floor in this *Jacques Courtens* interior was recovered from a castle. All the cabinetwork has been done in aged oak.

PP. 50-51

Wood throughout in this project by architect *Stéphane Boens*.

The sitting room of a seaside apartment, designed by *Polyèdre*. A nineteenth-century English writing desk in light pine. The table is an old serving tray in walnut.

A quest for refined forms in this country home: simple and refined at the same time. The art is by *Renaat Ivens*.

Two designs by architect *Bernard De Clerck*: above is a sitting room inspired by the eighteenth century; below is a more contemporary interior decorated by *Lacra*.

Architect *Stéphane Boens* masterfully integrates antique construction elements (a centuries-old wooden floor from *Rik Storms*) in a contemporary sitting room.

The sitting room in *Bernard De Clerck*'s spacious village home: the atmosphere it radiates is characteristic of the style of this renowned architect, who draws his inspiration from authentic and classic construction principles.

A project by architect *Vincent Van Duysen*. The walls were painted by *Kordekor*.

PP. 58-59

An old oak floor by *Corvelyn* in this villa, which has been
completely renovated by architect *Stéphane Boens*.

PP. 60-63

Three examples of the serene, sober style that characterises the interior designs by *Nathalie Van Reeth*.

A restful sitting area and library in a chalet in Verbier, created by interior designer *Nathalie Van Reeth* according to plans by the architects *Bruchez-Fellay*.

Furnishings from *Job Interieur* in this old mariners' inn: to the left are an upholstered footstool and a *Christi* settee; to the right is a *Huygen* settee with a detachable cover. Rayon curtains by *Métaphores*.

This sitting room has been decorated by *Inndekor*. Cotton blinds by *Shyam Ahuja*.

Works by artists including *Christo*, *Reinhoud* and *Arman* from *Guy Pieters'* contemporary art collection in an old farmhouse restored by architect *Stéphane Boens*.

Sophie Campion chose earth and caramel tones to harmonise with
existing elements (parquet, hearth) to give the light free play and to
create an intimate atmosphere. Art by *Antoni Tapies*. A bronze table by
Eric Schmitt for *Christian Liaigre*.

PP. 70-71

In the same house, a work by *Gerhard Richter* hangs above a
settee that is 3.2 metres in length. Two lamps by *Valentin
Manufactor* for *Liaigre*. The antique cabinets are from China.

The sage-green sitting room of a 1930s seaside villa, transformed and furnished by *Esther Gutmer*, who also designed the coffee table. The stools and the settee are by *Christian Liaigre*.

Chairs by *Poul Kjaerholm* and a work of art by *Jannis Kounellis* in a home transformed by *Pascal Van der Kelen*.

Mercure alchimique, a mixed-technique piece by *Sophie Cauvin*, above an *Actualine* settee. A bamboo opium table, cut to size by *Marc Vankrinkenveld*. To the left is a standard lamp by *Ateliers de la Cambre*.

Subtle nuances of colour in this creation by the late interior designer *Jean De Meulder*. The panelling is in tulipwood.

Two 'Thebes' stools by *Adolf Loos*. Tables in metal and treated bluestone.

PP. 76-77

The sitting room of a holiday home in Cadaqués, designed by *Baudouin Degryse*.

DINING ROOMS

The formal dining rooms of yesteryear have given way to the convivial rooms we know today. Nowadays, the dining room is a place where the whole family can come together, which is often integrated into a large open kitchen, and sometimes accommodated in an adjoining room.

A design by architect *Bernard De Clerck*. *Lacra* decoration: curtains by *Bisson Bruneel* and patinated chairs, covered with a *Sahco Hesslein* fabric.

View from the sitting room into the dining room in an interior designed by architect *Stéphane Boens*. Silk curtains by *Jim Thompson*, made up by *Lacra*. A taffeta tablecloth; the chairs are covered with fabric by *Canovas*.

The dining room of a historic
farmhouse, restored by *Stéphane
Boens*. The piece of art on the left
is by *Hans Hartung*.

Another *Boens* design. The aged oak floor is from *Corvelyn*.

PP. 86-87
An old milking parlour,
transformed into a dining room
by architect *Bernard De Clerck*.
The oak floor has been bleached;
the wall cupboards are original
eighteenth-century pieces. Table
and chairs by *Polyèdre*.

85

An interplay of white and brown tones in this sitting-cum-dining room. The napped blinds in a *Shyam Ahuja* fabric were made by *Inndekor*.

Greige North Sea tones in this 'dune house' by architect *Bernard De Clerck*. The dining table and chairs are by *Christian Liaigre*; the hearth wall was designed by the architect.

A 300 x 100 cm dining table by *Craeymeersch Project* in a house by architect *Marc Corbiau*. Chairs from the *Craeymeersch* collection, covered in a *Sahco Hesslein* fabric.

PP. 90-91
Contemporary transformation of a historic *hôtel de maître* in Antwerp by *Nathalie Van Reeth*. The original dining room and living room have been completely repainted; the existing parquet floor has been stripped and given a dark tint.

PP. 92-93
The custom-made units in this kitchen-cum-dining room are in untreated oak. An interior project by *Nathalie Van Reeth* in a house renovated by *Hubimmo*.

Nathalie Van Reeth separated this dining room from the living space with a simply designed fireplace. The Gustavian table and matching chairs are from the antique-dealer *Stéphane de Harlez* (Château de Deulin).

The wall paintings in an ancient castle have been restored to their former glory by *Hubert Coeman*. An interior design by *Marc Stellamans*.

A warm and sober dining room in a house by architect *Frank Van Laere*. The doors were made in *Francis Van Damme*'s traditional carpenter's workshop.

The dining room of *traiteur*
Christian Souvereyns.

A cosy corner with spacious storage cupboards, created by *De Menagerie* in a very narrow space (just 2.3 x 6 metres).

The original beams have been incorporated into the plan.

KITCHENS

In recent years, kitchens have undergone a real metamorphosis.
Under the influence of changing outlooks, developments in social circumstances
and the collapse of traditional family roles, the kitchen has gained a more varied purpose,
as a place for coming together, cooking, eating, working, and so on.
Individuality is the keyword for all the kitchen reports: a pleasant kitchen reflects the lifestyle
of the owners of the house and must be designed with their needs in mind.

Architect *Vincent Van Duysen* created this classic contemporary kitchen with its
La Cornue stove. The traditional tiles in white and light-grey tones are by
Dominique Desimpel.

The floor in this scullery consists of rows of cut bricks and reclaimed tiles.

Pages 108 to 113 show various kitchen designs by architect *Stéphane Boens*.

PP. 110-111 & 112A

The kitchen of this country house has a warm, minimalist atmosphere. Moroccan zeliges by *Dominique Desimpel*; a natural stone floor by *Deknock*. An *Aga* stove.

A terracotta floor and a worktop in exclusive marble. A design by *Stéphane Boens*.

A kitchen created by *Obumex* following a *Boens* design.

PP. 114-117

Following in the footsteps of the great architect *Raymond Rombouts, Group Moris* continues to build on the traditions of Flemish design: minimalist style and authentic materials.

The light streaming through this kitchen, designed by architect *Bernard De Clerck*, creates an inviting atmosphere. Furnishings in bleached solid oak and walls painted in pale lime-green. The beams have also been painted.

PP. 120-121

Four creations by kitchen designer *De Menagerie*.

This kitchen and washing area were designed by *Polyèdre*.
A reclaimed solid bluestone washbasin. The dining table is
also a *Polyèdre* design.

PP. 123-125

The cement tiles, which were originally laid in the servants' quarters of this impressive mansion, have been reclaimed for the kitchen. This kitchen occupies a large space, with ceiling-height cupboards and a display cabinet that *Francis Van Damme* constructed from old elements alongside a large mantelpiece and a professional stove.

The old Burgundian tiles in this kitchen have been arranged in a Roman pattern. A project by *Vlassak Verhulst*, the villa builders.

A symphony of white in the kitchen of sculptress *Mariette Teugels*: from the white Carrara marble floors to the white Delft tiles and the white *La Cornue* stove.

A picturesque village home in Damme has been restored in an authentic style by the former owners of *Kasimir's Antique Studio*.

A detail of the kitchen: *Corical* lime paints and zeliges from *Dominique Desimpel*.

A Buxy floor in a Roman design. The wall above the *La Cornue* stove has been clad

with dark zeliges. A *Themenos* design.

A kitchen in aged Flemish oak with a washbasin in solid Carrara marble. The sage-green colour of the furniture harmonises with the old tommettes on the floor. On the walls are authentic eighteenth-century tiles.

The simple and practical kitchen in this Spanish holiday home flows into the dining room. The floors are made from light terracotta tiles.

This vaulted kitchen, designed in a historic traditional farmhouse by architect *Bernard De Clerck*, is reminiscent of the half-underground cellar kitchens of early nineteenth-century manorhouses and famhouses with courtyards. The sink is in natural stone from the Lubéron.

This kitchen-cum-dining room, also designed by *Bernard De Clerck*, couples the utilitarian with the convivial. The dresser in the background was constructed from old panels by *Francis Van Damme*.

A distinctive and individual kitchen, designed by its owner. The floor is laid with reclaimed traditional tiles.

This *Tack* oak kitchen has been painted in olive and grey lime paints. The work surface is Jura stone. The stove is by *Lacanche.*

Modern art in a contemporary kitchen: *Objet Compressé* by *César* (1983).

Use of Basaltina lavastone throughout: for the flooring in the kitchen and indoor swimming pool, for the kitchen walls and the work surface in this minimalist design by *Filip Van Bever*. Natural stonework: *Van Den Weghe*.

The breakfast corner in a kitchen designed by *Esther Gutmer*. The table with invisible wheels was created by the interior designer; the hanging lamp is by *Christian Liaigre*. The beams and furnishings have been painted with *Agnès Emery* paints.

This kitchen in a former ambassador's residence from the 1920s was designed by *Fahrenheit*. The washbasins are surrounded with oak-plank furnishings. The work surfaces are in Aubergine stone, an Italian sandstone. The stools around the bar with its integrated *Lacanche* stove (*Fougeot* model) and the butcher's block are *Fahrenheit* designs. A cooker hood made from old glass and oak, equipped with halogen spotlights. Interior design: *Dominique d'Ursel* (*Les Petites Heures du Matin*).

A *Delaubrac Provençal 1600* stove in black and chrome with a gas oven, a small electric oven and a warming compartment, supplied by *Adek*. A *Costermans* design.

Simple lines and warm materials (a bleached oak parquet floor, solid natural stone as a work surface) in this contemporary kitchen, painted in lime by *de Waal*.

Alex Van De Walle's private kitchen: aiming for simple aesthetics, combined with patinated pieces, such as an English chair and an old mirror.

Christian Souvereyns' kitchen: simple furnishings around an *Aga* stove. Black Moroccan zeliges.

BATHROOMS

Over the years, bathrooms have gained an ever more important place in the house:
increasing amounts are invested in what has become a real spa culture - Jacuzzis
and whirlpools, water jets, huge bathtubs, saunas and steam baths, indoor swimming pools.
The possibilities are endless and ensure that contemporary bathrooms have become real bathing places.

PP. 146–149

All the cellar space (more than 100m²) is devoted to bathing and relaxing: Jacuzzi, bath, sauna, hammam and hydrojet.

Exceptionally large floor tiles in French whitestone (Massangis) were selected for this space. The walls also appear to be finished in Massangis, but this is deceptive: they have been painted with 'faux marbre' techniques that cannot be distinguished from real stone. The minimalist power of the largest room is further underlined by some unusual, well-chosen pieces, such as a nineteenth-century patinated cabinet from Sienna, a nineteenth-century taboret and a stone ball.

A bathroom designed by *Axel Vervoordt*, in particularly high-quality walnut supplied by *Rik Storms*. Painting: *Dankers Decor*.

A bathroom designed by *Axel Vervoordt* with a bathtub in old white marble.

PP. 152-153

The bathroom in the house of fashion designer *Edouard Vermeulen*, with furnishings designed by antique-dealer *Henri-Charles Hermans* from *Polyèdre* and clad in Belgian bluestone.

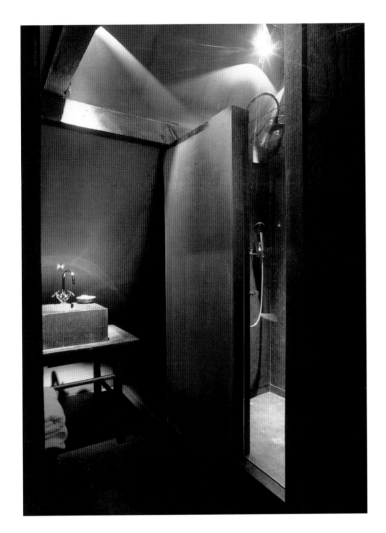

Two guest bathrooms in *Axel Vervoordt*'s castle at 's-Gravenwezel.

This bath has been fully clad with bluestone. The tap was reclaimed by *Polyèdre*.

The space available in this bathroom called for a sober and linear design. *Francis Van Damme* has turned old oak panels and hatches into distinctive bathroom furnishings. The oak floor is from France.

PP. 157-159

In an old countryhouse, architect *Bernard De Clerck* has designed an *en-suite* dressing room and bathroom with large custom-made oak cupboards, built in *Francis Van Damme*'s traditional carpenter's workshop.

PP. 160-163

Architect *Bernard De Clerck* transformed the half-submerged cellar under a countryhouse into a space for relaxation.

The original open, one-level cellar was remodelled to form a varied interplay of rooms on different levels, with vaulted ceilings, separated by arches and with new beams. The whole space was painted with pigmented marble lime.

The water zone in the relaxation space. *Dominique Desimpel* supplied the unfinished Moroccan tiles for the floor. The shower walls are clad with glazed zeliges. The stone washbasin is also from *Dominique Desimpel*. The taborets are of Chinese origin.

The shower area, with walls in Moroccan tiles. Torches in wooden pots.

Two designs by architect *Bernard De Clerck*. Floors in terracotta (photo above) and a chessboard design with old marble, supplied by *Rik Storms*.

Two *Group Moris* projects with very different white Carrara marbles. The panelling on pages 168 and 169 is made from oak.

A pinewood floor that was reclaimed from an old millhouse by architect *Xavier Donck*. Bath surrounds in Moroccan zeliges.

Taps and towel warmer by *Lefroy Brooks*.

PP. 172-173

Three very different bathroom projects by architect *Stéphane Boens*. Design (photo on the left, p. 172): *Brigitte Peten*.
Creation of the bathroom on p. 173: *Obumex*.

PP. 174-177

A bathroom and a handbasin in a house by architect *Bernard De Clerck*. The bathroom is finished in Luberon stone in bisque

shades. The painter added a pigment to the last layer of plaster in an evocation of traditional painting techniques.

A portrait of *Marie-Sophie Wilson* by the well-known photographer *Peter Lindbergh*, who is represented in Belgium by the gallery *Geukens & De Vil*.

These bathroom furnishings were made from hand-finished pine boards. Bath surrounds and washbasins in smoothed bluestone. Zeliges from *Emery & Cie*. Taps from *Lefroy Brooks*. A project by the interior designer *Catherine De Vil*.

The *en-suite* bathroom and bedroom in a design by *Nathalie Van Reeth*.

A bathroom designed by *Top Mouton* and created in bushhammered white Carrara marble by *Van Den Weghe*.

An indoor swimming pool in bluestone by *Saillart*.

A *Nathalie Van Reeth* project. The shower walls have simply been done in cement.

PP. 182-183
Sophie Campion chose smoothed Azur Valverde stone for the bath and washbasin surrounds. A floor in bleached oak and wall lamps by *Stéphane Davidts* (*Les Ateliers de la Cambre*).

A combination of metro tiles and natural stone in this shower designed by *Bernard De Clerck*.

This bathroom designed by architect *Bernard De Clerck* has a very calm, contemporary feel. The floor is in sandstone from the South of France with a gentle colour palette. The washbasins have been made from oak and tinted. The storage cupboards have been subtly concealed within the walls. The bath is free-standing, so that it does not overwhelm this relatively small space. The walls have been painted with lime, applied with a brush.

In this bathroom, an existing floor in the historic house has been reclaimed and arranged in a herringbone pattern. The bath has been clad with Belgian Rouge Royal marble. A project by *Francis Van Damme*.

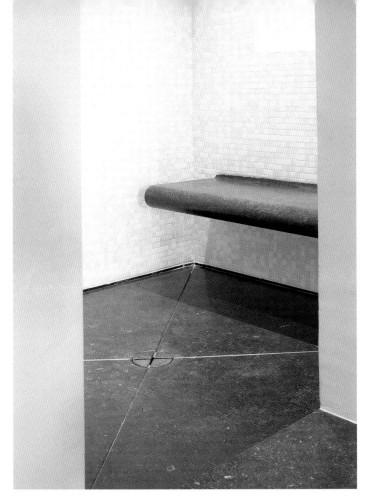

Three very different applications of Belgian bluestone: a water tank reclaimed by *Polyèdre*, a bench and shower floor by *Bruno Noël* and a hydro-jet created by *Baden Baden*.

Tap fittings by *Samuel Heath* (at *Lerou*). Shower cladding in white Carrara marble.

An old oak floor is combined here with painted cupboards and a surface in white Carrara marble.

Taps by *Volevatch* (at *Waterl'Eau*).

A shower room in Pompignan stone. Created by *Van Den Weghe* natural stoneworks.

A laundry with metro tiles from *Van Den Weghe*.

BEDROOMS AND DRESSING ROOMS

Nowadays, interior specialists and their clients attach a great deal of importance
to the design of bedrooms and dressing rooms.
The functions of sleeping and storage are often separated now, certainly where space permits:
en-suite bedrooms (with a separate dressing room) are increasingly popular.
Relaxation and recreation are also taken into account:
many bedrooms now have an extra sitting area with comfortable sofas and a separate TV room.

PP. 198-200

An interior project by *Bernard De Clerck* in a house that has been restored by *Guy De Moor* architects.

The hallway is painted in pale lime-green tones. Terracotta tommettes were chosen for the floor of the guests' dressing room. Cupboards with panels and latticework. In the painted wooden wall there is a 'Judas' window that makes it possible to look through into the corridor from the bedroom.

Page 200: the parents' dressing room, with its tall cupboards and solid-oak drawers. The walls, also in solid wood, have been painted.

A dressing room that has become a real living space. A project by *Bernard De Clerck*, constructed in the traditional carpenter's workshop of *Francis Van Damme*.

PP. 202-203

Subtle nuances of colour and harmony in this bedroom created by *Van der Voort Interiors*.

The warmth of wood in this project by *Christine Ceuterick – Bekaert*. Painting: *Group Kordekor*.

A design by architect *Vincent Van Duysen*. The *Kordekor* Group carried out the painting work with its bright white tints.

PP. 206-207

The bedrooms and dressing room of a chalet in Switzerland
designed by *Nathalie Van Reeth* in a project by *Bruchez-Fellay*
architects. The walls have been painted with lime; cabinetwork in
rough wooden beams and boards.

PP. 208-209
A hallway designed by architect *Stéphane Boens*.
The oak floor was reclaimed by *Corvelyn*.

A design by *Bernard De Clerck* architects. Curtain fabrics, bedclothes and headboard
by *Ian Sanderson*. Creation and fitting: *Arlette Gesquière*.

PP. 212-213

Three bedrooms in a renovated seaside villa. Left-hand page: this guest room has an oak floor. Behind the bed is a pinewood wine table. Picture above: the granddaughter's bedroom with its wool carpet and four-poster bed. Picture below: an eighteenth-century 'Protestant' Louis XV commode. An untreated pine floor.

Two dressing rooms designed and built in *Francis Van Damme*'s traditional carpenter's workshop.

To create an impression of more space, architect *Bernard De Clerck* designed a wooden wall with glass between the bedroom and the main bathroom. Lampshades and bedclothes by *Flamant*.

A design by architect *Xavier Donck*.

A bedroom designed by *Gert Voorjans*. A wool carpet by *BIC Carpets*. Linen curtains.

A hallway and old oak dressing room.

Cotton curtains from *Brunschwig & Fils'* 'Bengalai' collection. An *Abaca* carpet. A design by architect *Stéphane Boens*.

The blockprint fabric for the bed hangings was made by *Inndekor* and designed by *Christine Ceuterick* in a Rajasthani workshop (India). The hand-knotted carpet is by *DOC* (wool and silk). An oak floor by *Dubois*.

Two bedrooms designed by *Axel Vervoordt*: a guest room in the castle of 's-Gravenwezel and the parents' bedroom in an apartment in the centre of Antwerp.

This bedroom was designed by
Catherine De Vil. The oak cupboards in
the dressing room are on pivots. An old
reclaimed pitchpine floor. All the fabrics
are linen.

Three very different designs for children's rooms: a room with simple lines in Lasne, a romantic room in Uccle and a feeling of summer in a holiday home in Cadaqués (Spain).

A bedroom in grey tones by *Esther Gutmer*. Bedclothes by *Ralph Lauren*.

For a house in Knokke-Zoute, *Nathalie Van Reeth* selected parquet strip flooring in untreated oak.

A bedroom and dressing room in wengewood, designed by architect *Bernard De Clerck*. The floor is made from old, narrow oak planks.

The white bedroom of a seaside villa, designed by *Esther Gutmer*. Bedclothes and curtains by *Ralph Lauren*.

PP. 230-231

This bedroom, designed by *Sophie Campion*, is clad in teak and finished with pale-green tints in
linen, silk and cotton. Pieces of art by *Jose Maria Sicilia*, *Robert Mapplethorpe* and *Andreas Schön*.

SPACES FOR RELAXATION

The home has increasingly become a bastion that allows you to withdraw
from the hectic world and turn your back on everyday concerns.
However you relax (in your home cinema, reading a book or taking a siesta),
the design of these spaces is of increasing importance.

A successful combination of Azul Fatima stone and wengewood in this home cinema. The floor was supplied and laid by *Van Den Weghe*; interior design by *Obumex*. Painting by *Kordekor*.

In this duplex apartment, completely transformed and redesigned by architect *Pascal Van Der Kelen*, the bedroom and TV room are separated by large sliding doors.

The library shelves in this house designed by *Raymond Rombouts* have been painted with Corical paints. The cupboards have been made from old wood panels and painted with coloured latex paints.

Jean de Meulder (died in 2003) created a sense of space throughout this apartment. The classic doors have been replaced by sliding panels and the plinths have been removed. The sense of verticality has been strongly emphasised in order to create a whole that is more refined and sober. The monochrome painting is by *Renaat Ivens*; the sculpture is *LOVE* by *Robert Indiana*.

P.P. 242-243

The library and sitting room of architect *Xavier Donck*. In the foreground is a settee with a linen cover from *Actualine*. The white standard lamp is by *Christian Liaigre*.

SPACES FOR WORK

It is remarkable that working environments, where most of us spend the largest portion of our lives,
are still often treated like the poor relation.
The home office offers a contemporary solution: thanks to flexible working arrangements
and the technological revolution (high-speed internet connections, mobile telephones, wireless computer networks,
and so on) more people can set up working spaces at home. Their home offices show that living
and working can combine perfectly, providing the space is arranged in a creative and individual way.

A chair, table and lamp chosen by *Axel Vervoordt* in this writing corner.

The atelier/office of *Mark Moris* (*Group Moris*) with a typical Flemish fireplace and an oak ceiling.

Christine Ceuterick-Bekaert's workspace reveals her passion for the Far East. The office furniture, the lights and wall-lamps are all *Ceuterick* designs. In the middle of the library hangs a nineteenth-century wedding veil from the Punjab.

A home office designed by *Nathalie Van Reeth*.
Work surface in Eternit and inox. A *Van Severen*
desk and an *H20* chair for *Bulo*.

Another *Nathalie Van Reeth* design. Desk in rough, untreated oak.

The home office of engineer-architect *Alex Van De Walle* in a house dating back to 1742.
The large piece of art is by *Alex Dumont*. A *Tolomeo* desk lamp (*Artemide*).

The attic office of a holiday home in Knokke, designed by architect *Bernard De Clerck*. An antique Napoléon III *chauffeuse* chair and a Louis XVI-style desk chair. Built-in cupboards in painted wood. The door with its small window is a reclaimed piece.

PP. 256-259

Three offices designed by *Obumex*: an intimate, refined style.

A library design in pine by *Christine Ceuterick*. A *Milleraies* carpet.

An intimate workng atmosphere in the office of the Bruges antique-dealers *Brigitte and Alain Garnier*.

A doctor's office, placed at a key point between the examination rooms and the private rooms. A design by architect *Xavier Donck*.

A *Job* chair and an old oak table from interior design agency *Zon van Duurstede*. Wall-lamp by *Modular Lighting*.

A design by *Esther Gutmer* in an authentic mansion in Brussels. The leather desk and the chairs are from *Poltrona Frau* (*CEO desk*).

The panelling is in oak. Sofas from *Ralph Lauren*, covered with linen. The desk lamp is also by *Ralph Lauren*. The lamp on the mantelpiece is by *JNL*.

The mahogany and glass table is a *Gutmer* creation. On the floor is a sisal carpet.

The private office of the late interior designer *Jean De Meulder*. Chairs by *Marcel Kammerer* and an exclusive solid-silver desk lamp by *Buquet*. The drawing on the wall is by *Sol Lewitt*.

AROUND THE HOUSE

Although this collection of books on the home has often placed an emphasis
on interior design and furnishings, the external aspect of the house has not been neglected.
Bearing witness to this are the many photos of façades, terraces, driveways,
paths, and such features, that have been reviewed over the years.

This building, in the middle of an extensive 60-hectare estate, has been restored by *Guy De Moor* architects.

The countryhouse consists of restored living quarters and an adjoining barn that has been adapted to correspond to the needs of a young family. Architect *Bernard De Clerck* was asked to determine the interior, the fabrics, the external woodwork and the atmosphere of the building. He made the most of the large space, turning it into a kind of loft, consisting of an entrance hall, a sitting room, a kitchen and a family room.

This authentic farmhouse in Damme has been expertly restored by architect *Bernard De Clerck* in the style of the old Bruges farmhouses, in terms of both the design and the choice of materials. The garden was designed in collaboration with *André Van Wassenhove*.

PP. 274-275

Two countryhouses designed by architect *Stéphane Boens* that appear to have been there for centuries, but which have in fact only recently been built. The use of old construction materials creates a timeless atmosphere.

PP. 276-277

The magnificent garden of an old brewery, restored by

Michel en Christine Ceuterick-Bekaert.

PP. 278-279

Two designs by architect *Stéphane Boens* that show the consistent use of reclaimed materials (such as bricks, tiles and slates, bluestone and clinkers).

PP. 280-281

Continuation from page 279: exterior details of an English-inspired countryhouse created by *Stéphane Boens*.

PP. 282-283

The country style of *Group Moris*: the timeless beauty of historic construction materials (such as old cobbles, Balegem stone and bluestone and weathered oak gates).

PP. 284-285

A poolhouse in oak and reclaimed tiles, created by *Heritage Buildings*.

PP. 286-287

Architect *Frank Van Laere* restored an old millhouse, turning it into a distinctive summerhouse and swimming pool area.

PP. 288-289

Architect *Bernard De Clerck* designed a distinctive countryhouse in magnificent natural surroundings with a swimming pool and a landscaped pond. He also designed the garden, landscaped by *Group Moris*, as an extension of the house. For example, the large solitary box bushes (around twenty years old) were supplied and planted by *Moris*.

The flooring around the swimming pool is made of Dolphur, combined with Dutch clinkers. The pool itself is clad with grey Marathi marble. A design by *Van Den Weghe*.

A shed designed and created by *Group Moris*.

A terrace in old Balegem stone, supplied by *Rik Storms*.

The bangkirai wood terrace of *Mill Lodge*, a large countryhouse near Ghent that has been restored by architect *Xavier Donck*.

A creation by *Van Huele*, a dealer in old construction materials: sandstone cobbles and old oak gates, reclaimed from French military barracks.

IN THE GARDEN

In the two editions of *Jardins Intemporels* (*Timeless Gardens*, published in 2001 and 2003),
particular attention was paid to the garden as an important element of the landscape
and also to its place within that landscape: the featured gardens are in complete harmony
with the house and the surroundings. They are often gardens with a history, now occupied and enjoyed
by passionate gardeners and pleasure-lovers: conviviality, authenticity and simplicity are the keywords.

A shed designed by *Jacques Courtens*: the framework is made from old oak, the planks are afzelia wood.

Three custom-built greenhouses by *Group Moris*.

Two swimming pools perfectly integrated into
the surrounding landscape.

Two swimming pools in Provence.

PP. 304-305

An old carriage house has been transformed into a poolhouse by *Frank Van Laere*. Garden design by *Ludo Dierckx*.

The topiary 'clouds' create a harmonic transition from the formal garden and the swimming pool and the wood lying to the rear. Creation and landscaping: *Avantgarden.*

WEBLINKS / E-MAIL

(UPDATE 01/2005)

18-19	www.groepmoris.com
	www.arteconstructo.com (Corical)
19	francis.vandamme@skynet.be
20	Hommage Raymond Rombouts: www.betaplus.com
21	bernard.de.clerck@c3a.brenda.be
	www.rikstorms.com
22	www.vincentvanduysen.com
23	www.vandenweghe.be
24	www.polyedre.be
25	www.gertvoorjans.com
26-27	stephane.boens@skynet.be
	www.rikstorms.com
28-29	michel.ceuterick@pi.be
	christine.ceuterick@pi.be
30	x.donck@donck-en-partners.be
	www.garnier.be
31	dewaal@online.be
32	stephane.boens@skynet.be
33	www.saillart.be
40-47	www.axelvervoordt.be
41	dankers.decor@pi.be
48	stephane.boens@skynet.be
49	axel.pairon@skynet.be
50-51	www.polyedre.be
52-53	www.geukensdevil.com (Renaat Ivens)
54	bernard.de.clerck@c3a.brenda.be
	www.lacra.be
55	stephane.boens@skynet.be
	www.rikstorms.com
56	bernard.de.clerck@c3a.brenda.be
57	www.vincentvanduysen.com
	www.introkor.com (Kordekor)
58-59	www.corvelyn.be
	stephane.boens@skynet.be
60-64	nathalie.vanreeth@yucom.be
66-67	www.inndekor.com
68	stephane.boens@skynet.be
69-71	sophie.campion@skynet.be
	sales@christian-liaigre.fr
72-73	e.gutmer-meg@skynet.be
	sales@christian-liaigre.fr
74	www.pascalvanderkelen.com
	www.sophiecauvin.com
84	bernard.de.clerck@c3a.brenda.be
	stephane.boens@skynet.be
	www.lacra.be
	www.sahcohesslein.com
	www.jimthompson.com

217	www.gertvoorjans.com
	www.biccarpets.com
219	stephane.boens@skynet.be
220	christine.ceuterick@pi.be
	www.doc.be
221	www.axelvervoordt.be
222-223	catherine@omnibis.be (Catherine De Vil)
226	nathalie.vanreeth@yucom.be
227	e.gutmer-meg@skynet.be
228	bernard.de.clerck@c3a.brenda.be
229	e.gutmer-meg@skynet.be
230-231	sophie.campion@skynet.be
238	www.vandenweghe.be
	www.obumex.be
	www.introkor.be (Kordekor)
239	www.pascalvanderkelen.com
240	www.arteconstructo.com (Corical)
242-243	x.donck@donck-en-partners.be
	sales@christian-liaigre.fr
250	www.axelvervoordt.be
251	www.groepmoris.com
252	christine.ceuterick@pi.be
253	nathalie.vanreeth@yucom.be
	www.bulo.com
254	www.artemide.com
255	bernard.de.clerck@c3a.brenda.be
256-259	www.obumex.be
260	christine.ceuterick@pi.be
261	www.garnier.be
262	x.donck@donck-en-partners.be
264	www.poltronafrau.com
	e.gutmer-meg@skynet.be
	www.jnl.be
272-273	bernard.de.clerck@c3a.brenda.be
274-275	stephane.boens@skynet.be
276-277	christine.ceuterick@pi.be
	michel.ceuterick@pi.be
278-281	stephane.boens@skynet.be
282-283	www.groepmoris.com
284-285	www.heritagebuildings.be
288-289	bernard.de.clerck@c3a.brenda.be
	www.groepmoris.com
290	www.vandenweghe.be
	www.groepmoris.com
291	www.rikstorms.com
292	x.donck@donck-en-partners.be
293	www.vanhuele.be
301	www.groepmoris.com
304-305	www.ludo-dierckx.be
306-307	www.avantgarden.be

PUBLISHER

BETA-PLUS
Termuninck 3
B - 7850 Enghien
TEL.: 0032 (0)2 395 90 20
FAX: 0032 (0)2 395 90 21
Internet: www.betaplus.com
betaplus@skynet.be

PHOTOGRAPHER
Jo Pauwels

DESIGN
Polydem - Nathalie Binart

TEXT
Wim Pauwels

ENGLISH TRANSLATION
Laura Watkinson

ISBN
English version (TIMELESS LIVING 1995-2005)   9077213368

D/2004/8232/14

NUGI 648-656